SQUADRON

No. 2

The Republic
Thunderbolt Mk. I

Phil H. Listemann

ISBN: 978-2918590-36-1

Copyright

Revised 2018

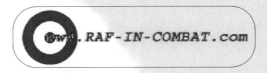

Colour profiles: Gaetan Marie/Bravo Bravo Aviation

Contributors & Acknowledgments:
Hugh Halliday, John Hamlin, Drew Harrison, Paul Sortehaug, Andrew Thomas.

PERSONEL :

(AUS)/RAF: Australian serving in the RAF
(BEL)/RAF: Belgian serving in the RAF
(CAN)/RAF: Canadian serving in the RAF
(CZ)/RAF: Czechoslovak serving in the RAF
(NFL)/RAF: Newfoundlander serving in the RAF
(NL)/RAF: Dutch serving in the RAF
(NZ)/RAF: New Zealander serving in the RAF
(POL)/RAF: Pole serving in the RAF
(RHO)/RAF: Rhodesian serving in the RAF
(SA)/RAF: South African serving in the RAF
(US)/RAF - RCAF : American serving in the RAF or RCAF

RANKS

G/C : Group Captain
W/C : Wing Commander
S/L : Squadron Leader
F/L : Flight Lieutenant
F/O : Flying Officer
P/O : Pilot Officer
W/O : Warrant Officer
F/Sgt : Flight Sergeant
Sgt : Sergeant
Cpl : Corporal
LAC : Leading Aircraftman

OTHER

ATA: Air Transport Auxiliary
CO : Commander
DFC : Distinguished Flying Cross
DFM : Distinguished Flying Medal
DSO : Distinguished Service Order
Eva. : Evaded
ORB : Operational Record Book
OTU : Operational Training Unit
PoW : Prisoner of War
PAF: Polish Air Force
RAF : Royal Air Force
RAAF : Royal Australian Air Force
RCAF : Royal Canadian Air Force
RNZAF : Royal New Zealand Air Force
SAAF : South African Air Force
s/d: Shot down
Sqn : Squadron
† : Killed

CODENAMES - OFFENSIVE OPERATIONS - FIGHTER COMMAND

CIRCUS:
Bombers heavily escorted by fighters, the purpose being to bring enemy fighters into combat.

RAMROD:
Bombers escorted by fighters, the primary aim being to destroy a target.

RANGER:
Large formation freelance intrusion over enemy territory with aim of wearing down enemy fighters.

RHUBARD:
Freelance fighter sortie against targets of opportunity.

RODEO:
A fighter sweep without bombers.

SWEEP:
An offensive flight by fighters designed to draw up and clear the enemy from the sky.

THE THUNDERBOLT I

In mid-1943, the RAF was facing a major challenge, as it needed to find a successor to two single-engined aircraft types, the Hawker Hurricane and the Curtiss Kittyhawk. Both were then being used with success as fighter-bombers but, at the same time, both had reached the limits of their development. The Hurricane was employed in the all major theatres, Europe, the Mediterranean and the Far East, while the Kittyhawk was serving in only the Mediterranean. In Europe, use of the Hurricane as a front-line aircraft was about to come to an end with the introduction of the Typhoon. For the two other theatres – the Mediterranean and the Far East – the problem remained unsolved as the Typhoon proved to be unsuitable in hot climates. The Allies, meanwhile, were planning how to terminate the war, which must in any event involve massive air offensives.

When the tropical tests carried out by the Typhoon in North Africa in 1943 showed unsatisfactory results, other types needed to be found. Only the Americans could help. Two US fighters were available at that time, the Merlin-powered North American Mustang and the Republic Thunderbolt. Because the USAAF was then in the process of increasing its strength by raising the number of fighter groups under its command, both types were reserved to equip USAAF groups first. The RAF, therefore, could not obtain the desired quantity of aircraft, especially in the case of the Mustang for which the RAF had a clear preference. This was also true of the American forces, which was somewhat ironic considering the Mustang was an aircraft they did not want at first because its design hadn't been initiated for the USAAF. While the British were able to get some Mustangs for their squadrons, the number allocated was insufficient to re-equip all the units and priorities for re-equipment were therefore set out. The RAF needed long-range escort fighters, a task the Spitfire could not fulfil in full, so the UK-based Air Defence of Great Britain (ADGB) and 2nd Tactical Air Force (2 TAF) squadrons received priority on the Mustangs, leaving only about one third of the allocations to be used in other theatres. As the threat of the Luftwaffe was seen as being more dangerous than the Japanese air arms, the Mustangs not required for UK-based squadrons were consequently sent to the Mediterranean where they began to re-equip Kittyhawk squadrons. In the case of the Hurricanes, the problem had to be solved by selecting the Republic Thunderbolt. Initially, the RAF was ready to purchase some of these fighters, though the numbers were expected to be low. This was not how it turned out...

The RAF's reluctance regarding the Thunderbolt stemmed from the first tests conducted by the RAF. In 1942, as with many other American aircraft, the RAF had tested the P-47. The variant tested was the B model, which was known to have a lot of shortcomings and was never actually used in operations. Even then, if the RAF had wanted to introduce the Thunderbolt into its inventory, the

The Thunderbolt assembly line at Republic's Farmingdale (NY) factory with the first RAF aircraft in the foreground. The Thunderbolts were not painted in the RAF's Day Fighter Scheme as the Americans did not have a stock of British paints. Instead, the colours were substituted with American equivalents - Olive Drab and Sea Grey with Light Grey for the under surfaces. They proved a very close match.

number of aircraft the US Government was ready to release was so small that it would have been totally impracticable to do so. By 1943 though, the P-47 had been significantly improved and the D model was in large-scale production. Moreover, the RAF had been witness to the first combat operations of the Thunderbolt in Europe, which were very encouraging. Furthermore, the P-47 was to become the backbone of the 9th Air Force, the USAAF's counterpart to the British 2nd TAF, which was then under formation, where the aircraft proved to be an efficient weapon as a fighter-bomber.

Thus, the idea was soon accepted that the Thunderbolt would succeed the Hurricane in the Mediterranean. This was felt to be logical, as the USAAF was introducing the 'Thun' as a fighter-bomber in the MTO by the end of 1943. The Thunderbolt was also earmarked as the successor to the Hurricane in the Far East, where the excellent long-range capabilities of the P-47 would be useful too. However, in Spring 1944 when the first Thunderbolts were shipped from the USA, the air war situation in Italy had changed and the Luftwaffe was no longer a major threat. The decision was therefore taken not to replace the Hurricanes with Thunderbolts, and eventually all the allocations for combat units were reserved for Far East units. That said, it must be also stated that for the RAF, the Thunderbolt was seen as an interim fighter-bomber, pending the availability of more Mustangs expected in 1945 or 1946, as the production was planned to increase considerably by this time. In other words, whatever good service the Thunderbolt could provide in the Far East, the countdown to its replacement had already started the day the first Thunderbolt reached India. It was scheduled to be withdrawn from use by the end of 1946.

THE MARK

The RAF used the only model open to foreign operators, the D model. However, it must be added that there were a lot of major differences introduced between the first production block and the last one. The RAF took charge of its Thunderbolts at the same time as the new block was put into production. Hence the RAF took charge of eight blocks, three designated the Mk.I, as follows:

P-47D-15-RE: This was the first block built (250 machines) with underwing pylons and plumbing within the wings to use underwing droppable fuel tanks. Only two were provided to the RAF, **FL731** and **FL732**, their respective US serials being 42-75788 and 75789.

P-47D-21-RE: This was based on the P-47D-20 which, compared to the D-15, had a new engine – the R-2800-59 (incorporating a new GE ignition system) – and also had a longer tail wheel strut, redesigned underwing pylons and heat ducted to the gun bay instead of electrical heaters. The D-21 was slightly different to the D-20 in having a redesigned throttle button that controlled the water injection. Of the 216 built, 57 were allocated to the British, **FL733-FL790**, but one (FL738) crashed on 31 January 1944 before delivery to the RAF.

A three-quarter front view of FL844, one of two Thunderbolts sent to the UK for evaluation. Note the 0.5-in calibre machine guns, a deadly and effective weapon arrangement.

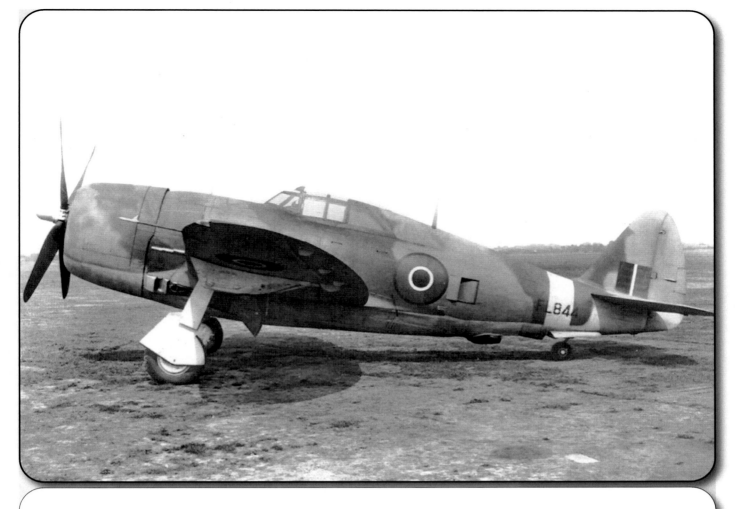

A side view of FL844. The Thunderbolt was a massive aeroplane compared to what the British pilots were used to. Those who converted from Hurricanes needed considerable flight time before totally mastering an aircraft almost twice the weight of the Hawker fighter.

P-47D-22-RE: The D-22 model was a D-21 with a new GE A-23 turbocharger and a different propeller, a Hamilton Standard Hydromatic of 13' 1 7/8" diameter in place of the Curtiss Electric 12' 2" model which equipped all the earlier versions. A total of 180 were delivered to the RAF, receiving the serials **FL791-FL850** (42-25639 to 25678 and 42-25779 to 25798), **HB962-HB999** (42-25799 to 25818 and 42-25914 to 25931) and **HD100-HD181** (42-25932 to 25953 and 42-26177 to 26236).

These first three blocks became the **Thunderbolt Mk.I** in the RAF inventory and, in all, 239 were delivered to the RAF between 29 February 1944 and 19 May 1944.

GENERAL USE OF THE THUNDERBOLTS BY THE RAF

While all the Thunderbolts were actually reserved for Far East squadrons, a handful of them were shipped to the UK to conduct various tests. Thus, two Thunderbolt Mk.Is, FL844 and FL849, found their way to the UK, and were test flown by the Aeroplane and Armament Evaluation Establishment (A&AEE) and various other test units in 1944 and 1945. The two Thunderbolt Mk.Is arrived in England in April 1944 and were used at the A&AEE (both) and AFDU (just FL849), until being stored at 51 MU in October 1945 for FL844 and January 1946 for FL849. They were eventually sold for scrap in March 1947.

In January 1944, the front line units in India Command/ACSEA comprised 12 Hurricane squadrons, mainly fighter-bombers. There was a programmed allocation of 60 Thunderbolts per month between January and June 1944, then 80 aircraft per month for the three following months. Taking wastage in training into account, the RAF could plan to convert eight 16-aircraft squadrons into Thunderbolts during the Monsoon season when air activity tended to decline. The remaining allocations from October 1944 onwards would only serve to maintain the operational squadrons. This was the case because the attrition rate was expected to be high regardless of combat losses, the tough climate and terrain hampering servicing at squadron levels. While repairs and aircraft salvage was possible in Europe, this was becoming difficult in Burma/India and many repairable aircraft were reduced to components due to a lack of the right facilities. This was useful in any event, as the Thunderbolts units had to face to recurrent shortage of spare parts. Nevertheless, many aircraft were abandoned as they were located in a spot where it would be uneconomical and hazardous for a salvage team to attempt to recover the aircraft.

At first, and to make things easier for the maintenance personnel, the squadrons were planned to receive their final allocation of either Thunderbolt Mk.Is or Thunderbolt Mk.IIs exclusively (though training could be carried out on both types at the same

A side view of FL839, at Farmingdale (NY), before it was shipped to the Far East. It served with 73 OTU in Egypt from July 1944 until 14 February 1946 when it was struck off charge.

time). However, some of the first aircraft to arrive in India seemed to have been corroded by sea water during shipment and many had to be cleaned up after being un-crated, something which took time. In fact, some were too badly damaged and were written off after inspection. Hence, at least eight Thunderbolt Mk.Is are known to have been written off due to bad corrosion (FL752, FL760, FL766, FL769, FL770, FL828, HB980 and HD150) while another, HB978, was simply written off as being too damaged during the crossing to consider repair. This left 229 Thunderbolt Mk.Is available for the units in Far East. Thus, the plans had to be changed on the basis of availability when the first squadrons became operational, and many had to go into combat with a mixture of Thunderbolt Mk.Is and Mk.IIs, the number of each mark varying from one squadron to another. Despite this, the attrition rate loss remained below earlier calculations and at the end of May, after the liberation of Rangoon, the RAF had 555 Thunderbolts on strength (including 173 Mk.Is), making the conversion of three more Hurricane squadrons possible, as well as enabling the withdrawal of the Thunderbolt Mk.I, in Spring 1945. Consequently, the Thunderbolt Mk.I disappeared from the front-line units by July 1945. As many Mk.Is needed to be overhauled after the last campaign launched to liberate Burma, most were struck off charge during the following weeks – the US didn't require them either. Apart from the examples flying in Egypt with 73 OTU and a handful with second line units in the Far East, by VJ-Day only around 50 were still held in flying condition in India and in reserve at MUs. With the war's end, the type was de facto declared obsolete and none were required to be returned by the US government. Before the end of September, 20 were already struck off RAF charge and the last were officially stricken on 28 March 1946 – a few were struck off charge later, the last two (FL777 and HD109) in May 1947, but this delay seems to have been an administrative entry only. All were scrapped in situ before the end of 1946. Generally speaking the 'T-Bolt' had the big advantage of having a radial, air-cooled engine which prevented the major troubles that liquid-cooled engines suffered in hot climates. It also had the long range that the Spitfire and the Hurricane lacked. In OTUs, the 'T-Bolt' was often chosen for these reasons, and the Spitfire didn't automatically win the pilots' favour. In a dogfight, the Thunderbolt was generally inferior to the Spitfire. As was sometimes said after training: 'Evasive action in a T-Bolt is taken by undoing straps and running round the cockpit'! In the Far East, the Japanese fighters were no longer a major threat when the Thunderbolt was introduced into service. In the tough combat conditions of the Far East, the pilots who had converted were quick to appreciate the qualities of the 'Thun'. Few had cause to regret the choice, and most liked the aircraft and were confident in its reliability and toughness. The pilots had a real preference for the Mk.II because of its bubble canopy, and were generally glad to give up the Mk.I for the Mk.II.

From the tactical point of view, the RAF within the 3rd TAF had split its units into two Groups, Nos. 224 and 221, for the two mains areas of land operations, Arakan and the Central (Imphal) Front respectively. The RAF reorganised and renamed its Wings on 1 October 1944 just after the Thunderbolt went into operations, and by the end of 1944, three wings were operating Thunderbolts sometimes incorporated with other aircraft types, mainly Hurricanes. The Thunderbolts squadrons moved from one Wing to another in response to local tactical needs. The Mk.I participated in only a single major campaign, the recapture of Burma, which started in December 1944 with Operation Capital and ended with the Operation Dracula, which led the way to the liberation of Rangoon in May 1945. Fewer than a dozen squadrons were equipped with Mk.Is, and only two, 5 and 135 Squadrons, were actually fully equipped with this mark during the period which ended with the liberation of Rangoon. One more squadron, No.146, converted to Mk.IIs in the final stages of the campaign in March 1945. All the others units used the Mk.I as an interim type pending the availability of the Mk.II and saw limited action with the Mk.I. In all, the figures of the Mk.I are modest, with fewer than 5,000 sorties and a single air-combat victory, compared to the 18,500 sorties flown by the entire Thunderbolt fleet.

TRAINING ON THE THUNDERBOLT

The first task the RAF had to carry out was to convert Hurricane pilots onto Thunderbolts. A special unit was formed on 20 June 1944 in 225 Group, No.1670 (Thunderbolt) Conversion Unit (1670 CU) which was based at Yelahanka in India. The first Thunderbolts were rapidly re-assembled and the unit was able to begin training of the first two unit selected, Nos.146 and 261 Squadrons immediately. The program was to continue to convert the units two by two. The unit used mainly Block D-21 Mk.Is during its short existence. While the groundcrew was trained on their aircraft, which was much more complicated than the Hurricane they were used to, the pilots had to follow a flight training programme comprising the following syllabus:

One sector recce and familiarisation flight
One section formation flight
Four Squadron balbo flights
One individual low level bombing flight
Two section low level bombing flights
Three 45 degrees dive bombing from 10,000 feet flight (releasing at 3,500 feet)
One air to ground firing flight
One air to air dogfight flight (with cine cameras)
One cloud flying flight
One low level cross country flight (400 miles)
One low level cross country flight (1,000 miles)

In all, that programme represented about 21-22 hours of flight completed with two hours on Harvards for instrument flying. Therefore, a Hurricane pilot should have been able to convert to a Thunderbolt in around 25 hours regardless of previous experience. This was easier said than done, as the Thunderbolt had a gross weight which was the double of the Hurricane. The Thunderbolt also had a propensity to spin, especially in the case of the Mk.II, which made things more difficult than expected, and many pilots found the Thunderbolt difficult to handle. Nevertheless, though many accidents occurred during the existence of 1670 CU, only three resulted in the destruction of the aircraft (HD171, FL767 and FL755 in that order), and only one in the pilot being killed (Sgt Peter R.C. Lapsley, a 20 year old Englishman from Manchester who was killed on his first solo on the type on 27 July 1944, flying Thunderbolt FL767). The aircraft was seen flying without difficulty at 6,000 feet when it was suddenly seen to be on fire, out of control and diving into the ground, leaving no chance of survival for the young pilot. It should be noted that of those three flying accidents, two (those involving FL767 and HD171), involved young Sergeant pilots

The units in charge of training on the Thunderbolt were given to experienced pilots. Left, S/L Patrick J.T. Stephenson of 1670 CU (later 8 RFU) had previously commanded 607 Sqn and been awarded the DFC. He was replaced by another 607 Sqn DFC recipient, S/L Lionel H. Dawes. For most of the Thunderbolt era, 73 OTU was commanded by G/C Frank R. Carey DFC and two bars DFM (right) who had fought in France, the Battle of Britain and Burma.

Date	Pilot	S/N	Origin	Serial	Code	Fate
13.07.44	Sgt Cyril E. AUSTIN	RAF No. 1672042	RAF	HD171		-
27.07.44	Sgt Peter R.C. LAPSLEY	RAF No. 1474375	RAF	FL767		†
17.11.44	Sgt Christopher L.W. BUTLER	RAF No. 1394016	RAF	FL755		-

Total: 3

during their first solo, suggesting that the Thunderbolt was far from easy to tame especially for pilots that had just graduated. The unit continued to convert pilots until 24 January 1945 when it was re-named No.8 Refresher Flying Unit (RFU) though it kept the same tasks, with the same codes, consisting of individual letters; known letters used by No.1670 CU by that time were FL736/N, FL748/W, FL754/V, FL761/D, FL762/B, FL764/F, FL771/U, FL772/J, and FL781/C. No.8 RFU inherited the Mk.Is from No.1670 CU, and later on some Block D-22-RE Mk.Is and Mk.IIs were added to the inventory in 1945. Having no more need to convert or refresh pilots for the decreasing number of Thunderbolt units, 8 RFU ceased to exist on 24 November 1945 and its personnel were posted to 3 RFU. The RAF rapidly took action to control the loss of aircraft and pilots, and safety measures were taken to avoid loss of pilots especially during the first flights. Hence, while 8 RFU had cause to deplore the loss of some 'T-Bolts', no incident resulted in the death of any pilot. Of the 15 Thunderbolts lost to accidents, nine were Mk.Is.

The unit continued to convert pilots until January 1945 when it was re-named No.8 Refresher Flying Unit (RFU) on the 24th keeping the same tasks, with the same codes – individual letters; known letters used by No.1670 CU by that time were FL736/N, FL748/W, FL754/V, FL761/D, FL762/B, FL764/F, FL771/U, FL772/J, FL781/C. No.8 RFU inherited the Mk.Is from No.1670 CU, and later on some D-22-RE Mk.Is and Mk.IIs were added to the inventory in 1945. Having no more needs to convert or refresh pilots for the decreasing Thunderbolt units, No.8 RFU ceased to exist on 24 November 1945 and its personnel posted to No.3 RFU. The RAF rapidly took actions to control the loss of aircraft and pilots, and safety measures were taken to avoid loss of pilots especially during the first flights. That is why if No.8 RFU had to deplore loss of T-Bolts, none conducted to the death of any of the pilots. Of the 15 T-bolts lost in accident, nine involved Mk.Is.

However, it is worth noting that, excepting the ground collision of FL754 with a Mk.II (KL247) and a ground test (HD107) accident, many of these incidents occurred during first flights, not to say the first solo (such as those involving FL736 and

Date	Pilot	S/N	Origin	Serial	Code	Fate
19.02.45	F/O William S.S. GARNETT	RAF No. 146115	RAF	FL762		-
28.02.45	W/C Alexander N. CONSTANTINE	RAF No. 40893	(AUS)/RAF	FL736		-
27.03.45	F/Sgt Charles R. RADFORD	NZ428300	RNZAF	FL754		†
10.04.45	Sgt Frederick C. LITTLEWOOD	RAF No. 1805264	RAF	FL733		-
24.05.45	Sgt William G. WAREHAM	RAF No. 1605629	RAF	FL789		-
27.06.45	Sgt Frederick G. MAYER	RAF No. 2210026	RAF	FL748		-
09.07.45	Sgt John L. EARNSHAW	RAF No. 1569354	RAF	FL796		-
11.09.45	Sgt Kenneth W. SOMERS	RAF No. 1608134	RAF	FL812		-
26.09.45	AC1 James R. FLANDERS	RAF No. 1637848	RAF	HD107		-

Total: 9

HD154, a Thunderbolt Mk.I, was allocated to 73 OTU during July 1944. It was struck off charge in March 1946.

FL762) before the pilots had learned the handling characteristics of the aircraft. It is interesting to note that in the case of the accidents involving FL736 and FL762, the pilots were both very experienced, with over 1500 hours logged in the case of W/C Constantine flying FL736 and close to 1100 hours in the case of F/O Garnett piloting FL762. Regarding the other accidents, mechanical problems were the main cause, as by this time the pilot's response had more or less adapted to the new aircraft. Thunderbolt FL812 was damaged by a ricochet during air-ground firing practice, but the pilot was able to return to base. As the type was close to retirement, no repairs were undertaken and the aircraft was declared Cat.E (not repairable) the same day. No.1670 CU, then 3 RFU, were two units formed to train pilots who usually already had operational experience, but in the short term, the RAF had to consider how to replace the pilots either lost in combat or in accidents, or arriving at the end of their tour. Therefore, new pilots fresh from training had to be trained on Thunderbolts to become available for operational requirements very quickly. No.73 OTU based at Fayid in Egypt provided training for Hurricane units in the fighter-bomber role for both Far East and Mediterranean theatres. Logically, as basically the missions remained the same, the Thunderbolt was added to the 73 OTU inventory at the same time that the Thunderbolt was entering RAF service. A mixed-type fleet of Thunderbolts were sent in Egypt once re-assembled in India, keeping the camouflage received at the factory in the USA. With the absence of any record, it is difficult to know how many Thunderbolts Mk.Is were actually sent to Fayid. There were around 30 at first, with arrivals starting in mid-summer 1944. A few more were added to the inventory in October 1944 once the initial training in India of the first squadrons had been completed. Later, when the Thunderbolt Mk.I was withdrawn from operational squadrons, half a dozen airframes, which didn't need any major overhaul in the short term, became available and were sent to Fayid to reinforce the existing Mk.I fleet at 73 OTU. During the ferry flight on 19 July 1945, HD175 was lost near Habbaniya in Iraq, and the pilot, W/O Roland W. Hall, was declared dead on admission to hospital. In all, it seems that around 40 Thunderbolt Mk.Is were put at the disposal of 73 OTU. The Mk.Is served until the OTU was disbanded on 25 September 1945 and the surviving aircraft were stored until all were struck off charge on 14 March 1946 and scrapped.

Thunderbolt Mk.I HD176 in flight over the Egyptian desert. It was one of the last of this mark to be allocated to 73 OTU in July 1944 and was struck off charge in March 1946. All of the Thunderbolts allocated to 73 OTU kept their American colours until repainting was required. However, it is not known which finish was applied to replacement aircraft that arrived during the summer of 1945. Did they keep their Temperate Land Scheme or were they painted in the Day Fighter Scheme. Either way, this must have been occurred in Egypt as, in 1945, the RAF had no stocks of Ocean Grey paint in India and it was not available in the Far East until the very last weeks of the war. It is also possible that replacement aircraft were cleaned of any paint and left in NMF as was the rule for Thunderbolts by the end of the war. No. 73 OTU only used numbers to identify aircraft and the unit marking generally consisted of an Ace of Spades card with a skull at its centre. The skull was normally white, but in some cases possibly yellow, perhaps indicating a flight identification colour.

Summary of the aircraft lost by accident - 73 OTU

Date	Pilot	S/N	Origin	Serial	Code	Fate
21.11.44	Sgt Aubrey DAVIES	RAF No. 1654041	RAF	FL805		†
06.01.45	Sgt Lawrence L. SMART	RAF No. 1809667	RAF	HD125		-
30.01.45	Sgt Richard A. WELLS[1]	RAF No. 772211	RAF	FL802		†
28.04.45	Sgt John J. CARSWELL	RAF No. 1568844	RAF	HD138		†
11.05.45	Sgt Fred D. IRELAND	RAF No. 1805964	RAF	FL829		-
12.06.45	Sgt Paul KENT	RAF No. 1806443	RAF	FL830		-
19.06.45	Sgt Ian MACDONALD	RAF No. 1570587	RAF	FL800		-
25.08.45	P/O Allan C.R. RIDD	RAF No. 163401	RAF	HD139		-
20.09.45	Sgt Mervyn D. STALLWORTHY	RAF No. 1675579	RAF	FL757		-

Total: 9

[1] Native of Calcutta, India.

Victories - confirmed or probable claims: *Nil*

First operational sortie:	Number of sorties: ca. 1,150
26.12.44	
Last operational sortie:	Total aircraft written-off: 12
15.05.45	

Aircraft lost on operations: 4
Aircraft lost in accidents: 8

Squadron code letters:
OQ

COMMANDING OFFICERS				
S/L James M. CRANSTONE	NZ405520	RNZAF	...	01.03.45
S/L Lionel H. DAWES	RAF No. 112699	RAF	01.03.45	...

SQUADRON USAGE

No.5 Squadron had considerable experience in the Far East when its personnel moved to Yelahanka in mid-September 1944 for conversion onto the Thunderbolt. Previously, they flew the Curtiss Mohawk, being one of the two operational units on that type, then Hurricanes. At that time, the Commanding Officer was S/L Cranstone, a New Zealander who had spent a long time fighting the Japanese, first with No.243 Squadron on Buffalos at Singapore, then with 67, 146 and 11 Squadrons on Hurricanes in Burma/India before joining 5 Squadron. He had been the squadron's commanding officer since June 1944. Training on the Thunderbolt Mk.Is began on 25 September, with a familiarisation flight for most of the pilots. It was not long before the first incident involving the destruction of an aircraft, the following day in fact. Flight Sergeant Michael W.N. Hart (RAAF) forgot to remove the pitot cover before taking off. Having no speed indication, the pilot failed to pull up in time and crashed at the end of the runway. Hart escaped major injuries, but FL819 was a total write-off. Training continued intensively until the end of the month, and close to 150 hours were logged on Thunderbolts. In October conversion continued and 450 hours were flown, but not without inci-

New Zealanders photographed about the time of the changeover to the Thunderbolt in September 1944. Left to right: F/O George I. Baines, W/O Euan R. Worts, Mrs and S/L J.M. Cranstone (CO), F/L Ralph H. 'Snow' Jenkins, P/O Raymond R.A. McLauchlan.
Baines, Worts and McLauchlan had served with the squadron for more than two years and were at the end of their tours so did not convert to the Thunderbolt. Jenkins did, having arrived in June 1944. He left one year later.
(J.M. Cranstone via Paul Sortehaug)

F/L William Souter, one of 5 Sqn's flight commanders in the autumn of 1944, prepares to start the engine of an early Thunderbolt. Souter was a long-serving member of the squadron having flown Mohawks and Hurricanes with it in 1942. He left in April 1945 to take command of 146 Sqn, another Thunderbolt unit. Very little information about the aircraft flown by 5 Sqn is given in the unit's Operational Records Book. Among the Mk.Is known to have been in service with the unit during September/October 1944 are: FL807, FL816, FL819, HB890, HD104, HD119, HD131 and HD132.
(J.M. Cranstone via P. Sortehaug)

dent. On the 18th of the month, F/Sgt John E. Stannard forgot to lower the undercarriage when returning from practice formation flying, and the subsequent belly landing wrecked his aircraft (HD180). Two days later, not one, but two more Thunderbolts were written off, both during an altitude climb to 37,000 feet during the afternoon. The Australian pilot of HD140, W/O Colin G. Turner, and his wingman, the Canadian W/O Maurice Huneault in HB983, became lost when cloud formed below them and fearing a shortage of fuel they decided to make a forced landing, which, fortunately, was successful for the pilots as they escaped injury. At the end of the month, the squadron moved to Cholavarum then to Kajamalai when training was completed despite the Monsoon; 500 more hours were logged in November. The squadron had 32 pilots in its ranks at that time, representative of much of the Empire, with five Australians, four Canadians, two New-Zealanders and one South African.

On 12 December, the squadron joined 905 Wing at Nazir south of Cox's Bazar to operate over Burma. Apart from a handful of Mk.II aircraft, the squadron was equipped with Mk.Is. However, due to a lack of equipment at Nazir, the squadron could not become operational until nearly the end of the month. The first operational sortie was carried out on the 26 December, the CO (flying Mk.II HD279) led three other aircraft on an escort for Dakotas in a supply dropping mission. The squadron then flew operations on every day of December, and most of the 98 sorties were done on Mk.Is, but not without cost. On the last day of the year, while returning from an escort mission, Sgt Graham Longhurst's Thunderbolt (FL809) ran into to P/O John M. Townsend's machine (FL825) on landing. Both aircraft were written off, but no personal injuries were reported.

In January, 700 hours were flown on operations, luckily without any loss, even though the availability of spares parts was a major issue. In over 350 sorties flown (most on Mk.Is), the squadron reported the destruction of four canoes, two sampans, one pagod and three bashas, and many more damaged. The only bad news for the month was the handing over of the Mk.IIs for old Mk.Is. Indeed, between 15 and 19 January 1945 in the afternoon, 258 and 5 Squadrons traded a part of their Thunderbolt complement, 5 Squadron inheriting the Mk.Is so they could eventually be totally equipped on that type. As the exchange had been planned since the beginning of the month, no major effort was made to maintain the Mk.II aircraft in flying conditions, priority being directed toward the Mk.Is instead. Furthermore, the Mk.Is coming from the 258 Squadron – FL792, FL806, FL807, FL814, HB984, HB991 and HD129 – had been flying with 258 Squadron since the beginning and so were in rather poor condition. By 19 January, only the CO retained a Mk.II and only until the end of the month. After that, the squadron flew exclusively on Mk.Is.

During the first ten days of February, the squadron was engaged in flying close support operations for 224 Group. The targets were mostly in the Kangaw area against prepared Japanese defensive positions. From 12 February, the squadron's task changed and it was now called upon to fly in indirect support by attacking targets for 221 Group, supporting the 14th Army. Bridges and airfields were at the top of the list of target to hit. After twelve days of such operations, the squadron returned to 224 Group but activity was limited while in support of the 82nd Division, and on 27 February, the unit returned to supporting 221 Group with the main task of destroying rail yards around Mandalay. In that month, over 200 sorties were carried out and 85 tons of bombs were dropped without a single loss, whether in operations or accidents. On the first day of March, S/L Cranstone relinquished command to S/L Dawes, who had flown with No.607 Sqn with which he had been awarded the DFC.

Even though the squadron's pilots complained about the Mk.I and were waiting impatiently for the long-promised Mk.II, serviceability remained high during March. This month the squadron was able to put an average of 13 aircraft into the air daily, and over 1,000 operational hours were recorded across over 300 sorties – during which 83 tons of bombs and over 136,000 rounds of ammunition were expended. Due to the fact the squadron had to attack targets far from its base, the pilots were obliged to use long range tanks. This was on top of the loss of three Thunderbolts over the month, one on the 13 March, two on the 14 March. On the former date, Lt John W. 'Jock' Cameron (SAAF) had the misfortune to experience the engine of his Thunderbolt, the last Mk.I delivered, HD181, cutting out at 500' just after take-off during a non operational flight. He tried to make an emergency landing on a beach, and succeeded in getting down with only superficial bruises and cuts, and mild shock. The Thunderbolt, however, broke into three pieces and was wrecked. The following day, the squadron ran out of luck when transiting to Sadaung from where they were to operate, as two Thunderbolts collided. This accident occurred when W/O Thomas B. Drake, stopped without leaving enough room after landing at Sadaung for the Thunderbolt behind, flown by F/O Arthur B. Skidmore (RCAF). Both aircraft were written off, but both pilots escaped injuries.

April started with patrols between 9.00 and 17.00 over the Pagan–Meiktila supply corridor, but it also opened with the loss of another Thunderbolt – FL809 – during such a patrol. The engine of FL809/Z started giving trouble to its pilot, F/Sgt John K. Cross, which obliged him to make a forced landing near Meiktila, fortunately without consequences for the pilot. Until that time, while the squadron had lost some aircraft either in accidents or operations, it had been without loss of life. Things changed on the 7th when F/Sgt Philip Anson was killed during a cab-rank mission. After having dropped his bombs and pulled out of his bombing dive, Thunderbolt HD112/D was seen to blow up and crash into the ground in flames. Twelve days later, 5 Squadron moved to Cox's Bazar though that move did not result in much activity. Not a single mission was carried out, and the only event worthy of note was the departure of F/L William Souter, on 20 April. Souter was one of the squadron's longest serving pilots, having flown there for over two years. He left to take command of another Thunderbolt unit, 146 Squadron. On 28 April the squadron moved to Kyaukpyu with the hope of carrying out more operations, but only one was recorded until the end of the month, an attack on Moulmein airfield on the 29th. The squadron claimed one Betty and one Tojo damaged on the ground. In all, in April the squadron dropped 31 tons of bombs and fired 71,000 rounds of ammunition over 110 sorties. May, the last month the squadron was engaged in operations, was rather busy, at least the first days which saw the liberation of Rangoon. Over 120 sorties were carried out, but on the 12 May, the day of their last sortie led by the CO, the pilots were informed that they would be transferred to 221 Group, information which was received with mixed feelings so close to the end of war. Instead, the squadron received orders to move back to Chakulia for withdrawal and re-equipment. On 15 May, a weather reconnaissance was flown by P/O David F. Michell and F/Sgt Huia C. Parker (RNZAF), marking an end to the operational use of the Thunderbolt Mk.I by 5 Squadron. Sadly, the squadron had one more loss to report on 2 June, when the engine of the aircraft flown by F/Sgt Ronald J. Tebby – HB984/S – failed on take-off for a training flight with napalm tanks. While the pilot tried to get back to the airstrip after having released his Napalm, the engine seized on approach, and being too low the aircraft hit a truck and the aircraft overturned. F/Sgt Tebby died later on in hospital. Four days later, the squadron moved back to Cox's Bazaar and, during July, the long promised Mk.II Thunderbolts eventually arrived to replace the war-weary Mk.Is.

Two Australian pilots during the Thunderbolt era 1944-1945. Left, William D. 'Blue' Williams of New South Wales served with 5 Sqn between May 1944 and August 1945, and, right, Ronald C. Henning from Queensland arrived one month later than Williams, but left in June 1945.

Summary of the aircraft lost on Operations - 5 Squadron

Date	Pilot	S/N	Origin	Serial	Code	Fate
31.12.44	Sgt Graham K. **Longhurst**	RAF No. 1387922	RAF	**FL808**	-	-
	P/O John M. **Townsend**	RAF No .162305	RAF	**FL825**	-	-
01.04.45	F/Sgt John K. **Cross**	RAF No. 1322591	RAF	**FL809**	OQ-Z	-
07.04.45	F/Sgt Philip **Anson**	RAF No. 1623027	RAF	**HD112**	OQ-D	†

Total: 4

The wreckage of FL809/OQ-Z. The engine of FL809 started giving trouble and forced the pilot, F/Sgt John Cross, to make a forced landing near Meiktila from which he emerged uninjured.

Summary of the aircraft lost by accident - 5 Squadron

Date	Pilot	S/N	Origin	Serial	Code	Fate
26.09.44	F/Sgt Michael W.N. **Hart**	Aus. 426096	RAAF	**FL819**		-
18.10.44	F/Sgt John E. **Stannard**	RAF No. 1318662	RAF	**HD180**		-
20.10.44	W/O Colin G. **Turner**	Aus. 408939	RAAF	**HD140**		-
	W/O Maurice R.R.J. **Huneault**	Can./ R.96945	RCAF	**HB983**		-
13.03.45	Lt John W. **Cameron**	SAAF No. 329086V	SAAF	**HD181**		-
14.03.45	W/O Thomas B. **Drake**	RAF No. 943911	RAF	**HD133**		-
	F/O Arthur B. **Skidmore**	Can./ J.16460	RCAF	**HD170**		-
02.06.45	F/Sgt Ronald J. **Tebby**	RAF No. 1586328	RAF	**HB984**	OQ-S	†

Total: 8

Victories - confirmed or probable claims: 1.0

First operational sortie:
16.10.44
Last operational sortie:
12.05.45

Number of sorties: ca. 1,250

Total aircraft written-off: 8

Aircraft lost on operations: 5
Aircraft lost in accidents: 3

Squadron code letters:
WK

COMMANDING OFFICERS				
S/L Leonard C.C. HAWKINS	RAF No. 102129	RAF	...	10.06.45

SQUADRON USAGE

This squadron was formed in England in August 1941 on Hurricanes, though it served for only a couple of weeks in the UK before being sent to Burma to reinforce the RAF in the region. However, it arrived at the worst possible moment, in January 1942 when the British were retreating from Burma. The first steps were rather chaotic but in the following months, the squadron was able to exist on its own. It was employed intensively between 1942 and 1944 flying Hurricanes over Burma. Early in May 1944, the unit, under the leadership of S/L Leonard C.C. 'Lee' Hawkins, was chosen to become one of the first two units to convert to Thunderbolts. The squadron was based at that time at Minneriya at Ceylon, and this new challenge was well accepted by the whole unit. Ground school began during the second week of the month and the first three Thunderbolt Mk.Is arrived on 17 May. The next day, the first flights were carried on by the CO and F/L Lewis. Two more Thunderbolt Mk.Is arrived on the 20th of the month, with four more arriving the following day. By the end of the month, over 200 hours had been flown, and all pilots had flown their new mount at least once. The squadron did, however, retain some Hurricanes to allow the pilots to fly on regular basis, and flights continued on this type during the month. In June, pilots continued to fly on both aircraft, and on 5 June, a fatal accident occurred (the first on an RAF Thunderbolt), when F/L 'Budd' Hart (RCAF) was killed while flying HB977. It seems that aircraft fell out of control, and it

S/L Lee Hawkins took command of 135 Sqn in March 1944 and subsequently led it throughout the unit's entire Thunderbolt era.
(Andrew Thomas)

A line-up of 135 Sqn Thunderbolts at Chittagong. Note the spinners of HB982/D and HD173/A are painted red to indicate their flight. The squadron code letters 'WK' were later added. The squadron went to war in October 1944 with: FL831, FL836, FL837, FL840, FL847, HB962, HB963, HB971, HB975, HB981, HB986, HD102, HD126, HD158, HD173 and HD175.

G/C G.F. Chater (OC 902 Wing) conferring with S/L Lee Hawkins, kneeling, and other pilots of the squadron. The aircraft have been newly-coded 'WK'. In the background, HB975/WK-L, usually flown by Hawkins, has five sortie markings forward of the cockpit. As the aircraft completed its fifth op on 25 October, and its sixth on the 28th, it is likely that this photo was taken between those two dates.

was thought that Hart became unconscious, probably due to an oxygen failure during a climb to 37,000 feet. Otherwise, the squadron continued its training on Thunderbolts, and close to 500 hours were flown that month. In July, the lack of spare parts for the Thunderbolts affected seriously the training, and only 140 hours were accomplished and little flying was carried out after the 12th of the month. In August things were even worse, with only 40 hours flown. Training was completed by early October and the squadron was sent to Chittagong in India to start operations, being fully equipped with Thunderbolt Mk.Is. During that time, 135 Squadron lost another Thunderbolt (FL837) on 1 October, when Lt Henry Briscoe (SAAF) made a forced-landing on a road after running short of fuel due to becoming lost, but he escaped injury.

The first operation was recorded on 16 October when eight Thunderbolts took off at 10.10 to strafe a Japanese position in the Foul Point area. The mission was successful – about 50 bashas were strafed, and the formation did not meet any opposition. Until the end of the month, 68 other sorties were carried out, but sadly the squadron recorded its first lost when on the 28 October, Sgt Stevens stalled just after take-off and crashed, being killed instantly. This flight was the first carried out with drop tanks, and it is possible that the pilot, lacking in experience, put his aircraft, HB962, in a dangerous position from which he could not recover. In November operations continued and on the 3rd of the month, the squadron participated to Operation 'Eruption' – strafing Mingaladon airfield. The squadron returned safely even though the aircraft flown by F/O John P. Rykens (FL847) was hit by flak. On 17 November, the squadron was called to provide an escort to Liberators bombing Rangoon. The target was successfully bombed and the pilots went into action against Japanese fighters which tried to intercept the formation. The Thunderbolts engaged in combat, and after ten minutes W/O Robert E. Windle and F/Sgt Robert E. Maxwell shared the destruction of a Ki-43 Oscar, while P/O Peter J. Anson and F/Sgt Frederick W. Hammond were also able to fire at the enemy aircraft, but only Hammond was able to claim another Oscar damaged. This became the only air-to-air kill recorded by an RAF Thunderbolt Mk.I during its entire career with that air force! Otherwise, the rest of the month was uneventful and just over 100 sorties were completed.

There were no operations for the first ten days of December. By that date, the squadron was based at Jumchar and was part of 902 Wing, flying with another Thunderbolt unit, 30 Squadron. Operations resumed on 13 December and 165 sorties were carried out during that month, mainly sweeps, patrols and escorts. It was during such a mission, a VIP escort, that the squadron lost two more Thunderbolts; HB982, flown by the now famous P/O Windle, collided with HB963 flown by Sgt John E Hargreaves in flight at 10,000 feet. The latter had no alternative but to bale out, though Windle was able to return home. However, his aircraft was written off, being declared beyond economic repair. On a more positive note, the squadron was happy to receive notification that a well-deserved DFC was to be awarded to the CO, S/L Hawkins, gazetted the previous month. It was only the second DFC for the squadron after two and a half years of fighting! It should be noted that units in Far East were sometimes neglected when it came to awards. January was a busy month with close to 250 sorties carried out against a great variety of targets; 212,000 lbs of bombs were dropped and about 250,000 rounds of 0.50in ammunition were fired. The squadron dropped also dropped the then-new Napalm incendiary bombs. The only concern about the use of these bombs was the need to reduce speed below 300mph to drop them, meaning that the aircraft was more vulnerable to flak during that phase of flight. Morale in 135 Squadron remained high, reinforced by the fact that no losses, whe-

P/O Robert E. Windle, left, and F/Sgt Robert E. Maxwell, the two pilots who, on 17 November 1944, shot down a 50th Sentai Ki-43 to claim the only Thunderbolt Mk.I victory. *(via Andrew Thomas)*

ther operational or accidental, were recorded. Nevertheless, maintenance continued to be a major issue, and at one point, the number of aircraft available dropped to eight, or half of the unit. That was mainly because of the high flying hours on each Thunderbolt (between 170 and 200), and the CO was lobbying for newer Mk.Is or, preferably, a change to the Mk.II with its bubble canopy. Many pilots had complained about the poor visibility offered by the canopy used on the Mk.Is. Actually, though it was not said directly, many hoped to see the Mk.I removed from operational service. As for the pilots, the CO complained of a lack of training of the new and replacement pilots, many being below the average standard, and the latter could not be sent on operations, while many experienced pilots were reaching the end of their tour. Due to the lack of available aircraft, training could not be undertaken and some new pilots were consequently grounded. In February, the overall situation hadn't changed much, but the squadron was able to carry out 270 sorties, a record in terms of its use of the Thunderbolt so far. However, one Thunderbolt, HD102, was lost on 19 February in an accident. The aircraft, which belonged to the detachment base at Cox's Bazar, took off for a non-operational flight. One tyre burst, causing the Thunderbolt to swing off the runway and crash. The pilot, F/O Windle escaped injuries but the aircraft was a write-off. In March and April 1945, little changed except that the problem regarding pilots had worsened, as many of the section leaders were close to tour-expired and nobody was available who could replace them. Also, the squadron saw the arrival of number of NCOs, freshly graduated but far from ready to fly operationally, and almost no officers. By March the squadron was chronically short of officers of all ranks. Despite this, 135 Squadron completed over 340 sorties in a month and a half until operations stopped on 13 April to prepare the move to Akyab in Burma for Operation 'Dracula', from 24 April. One loss was recorded during the period March-April, when W/O Dennis R. Whiskin, a Canadian from British Columbia serving with the RAF, was posted missing from a mission on 28 March during a strafing sortie. He was last seen flying south of the target at 700 feet. In March alone, over 190,000 lbs of bombs were dropped, 170,000 rounds of 0.50 expended and 90 Napalm tanks dropped in missions against the Japanese. Sorties resumed on the first day of May and the next day, the squadron lost HB981/H flown by F/Sgt Fergus M. Hutchinson when he failed to get airborne during take-off. Hutchinson attempted to stop the Thunderbolt but overshot the end of the strip and ground looped, without any major consequences for the pilot. The last operations took place on the 12 May when eleven Thunderbolts led by the CO took off at 8.00 to strafe and bomb Japanese positions at Bawgaligiy. The aircraft remained over the target for 10 minutes before returning to base. Five day later, the squadron left Akyab for Chakulia (India) where the squadron was supposed to trade its war-weary Mk.Is for brand new Mk.IIs. Nature intervened at that point – 135 Squadron was struck by a big gale which destroyed among others, some of the remaining Mk.Is, including FL798, HB966, HB975, HD108, HD134, HD135, HD146. Two more (FL834 and FL836) were slightly damaged but not repaired as the type was about to be removed from service. When the unit was renumbered as 615 Squadron on 10 June 1945, it is believed that no more Mk.Is were still in the squadron's hands.

F/Sgt Standish Walker in October 1944 climbing into a Thunderbolt Mk.I that has three mission markings. He is wearing his Tropical Survival Suit, Mae West, and is carrying a jungle knife and screwdriver in a leg scabbard, all standard equipment for a fighter pilot in the region.

Claims - 135 Squadron (Confirmed and Probable)

Date	Pilot	SN	Origin	Type	Serial	Code	Nb	Cat.
17.11.44	P/O Robert E. **Windle**	RAF No. 173807	RAF	Ki 43	**HB982**		0.5	C
	F/Sgt Robert E. **Maxwell**	RAF No. 1337454	RAF		**HD124**		0.5	C

Total: 1.0

Summary of the aircraft lost on Operations - 135 Squadron

Date	Pilot	S/N	Origin	Serial	Code	Fate
28.10.44	Sgt Paul H. **Stevens**	RAF No. 1604434	RAF	**HB962**		†
15.12.44	P/O Robert E. **Windle**	RAF No. 173807	RAF	**HB982**		-
	Sgt John E. **Hargreaves**	RAF No. 1623540	RAF	**HB963**		-
28.03.45	W/O Dennis R. **Whiskin**	RAF No. 1314711	(CAN)/RAF	**HD158**		†
02.05.45	F/Sgt Fergus M. **Hutchison**	RAF No. 1522717	RAF	**HB981**	WL-H	-

Total: 5

Summary of the aircraft lost by accident - 135 Squadron

Date	Pilot	S/N	Origin	Serial	Code	Fate
05.06.44	F/Lt Elton B. **Hart**	CAN./ J.7903	RCAF	**HB977**		†
01.10.44	Lt Henry **Briscoe**	SAAF No. 329200V	SAAF	**FL837**		-
19.02.45	F/O Robert E. **Windle**	RAF No. 173807	RAF	**HD102**		-

Total: 3

Also, destroyed by gale of 23.05.45 at Chakulia, the following Mk.Is are belived to be still in squadron hands: FL7978, HB966, HB975, HD108, HD134, HD135, HD146, not counting FL834 & FL836 which not repaired owing to the withdrwal of the type.

Victories - confirmed or probable claims: Nil

First operational sortie:
16.09.44
Last operational sortie:
13.03.45

Number of sorties: ca. 1,685

Total aircraft written-off: 8

Aircraft lost on operations: 4
Aircraft lost in accidents: 4

Squadron code letters:
NA

COMMANDING OFFICERS

S/L Lawrence M. O'LEARY	RAF No. 41728	RAF	...	22.10.44
S/L Raymond A.C. WEIR	RAF No. 119839	RAF	22.10.44	...

SQUADRON USAGE

No.146 Squadron was formed in 1941 just before Japan entered into war, and served since then in the Far East flying Hurricanes from India. This lasted until 15 May when the last sorties on that type were recorded. The next month, while under the command of S/L Lawrence M. O'Leary, the squadron was selected to become one of the first two units to convert onto the Thunderbolt Mk.I. After having carried out the cockpit checks, the first solos were recorded on 21 June. During the first week, the number of flights remained low with an average of three or four per day, but from 28 June onwards, things became more intense and between 10 and 17 training flights per day were carried out as far as the weather permitted. By the end of the month, over 50 hours on Thunderbolts had been completed. At the beginning of July the Thunderbolts were grounded for two days due to mechanical troubles but flights resumed on the 3 July and training intensified during the next few days, with over 30 hours completed by 15 July. Sadly, two days later the squadron lost two aircraft, when F/L Terrence B. Marra (RNZAF), B Flight leader piloting HD101, and F/O Livingstone A.W. Kerr in FL744, collided in flight while practising formation flying. Owing to damage to an aileron Marra was obliged to bale out from his Thunderbolt while Kerr was able to make a perilous emergency landing after having entered into spin only to recover at 500 feet! He was able to land safely but roughly; FL744 was first categorised A.C. but was later declared irreparable and reduced to components. Marra was knocked out when he struck the ground, but suffered only superficial injuries and recovered quickly. Training continued until it was stopped on 28

'Terry' Marra, a New Zealander, served with the squadron from May 1942 until tour-expired in October 1944. Marra was a former Buffalo pilot with 243 Sqn at Singapore where he claimed one confirmed victory. He was later briefly attached to Nos. 258 and 232 Sqns, prior to the fall of the island, before his attachment to 488 (NZ) Sqn and the 2nd Dutch Buffalo Squadron in Java. Repatriated to Ceylon, he was posted to 67 Sqn in April 1942 before joining 146 Sqn.
(via Paul Sortehaug)

No. 146 Squadron was among the first two fighter units that converted to Thunderbolts. Initially, aircraft were allocated to pilots. FL848 was flown by F/O Edgar N. Wilson (RNZAF). This practice had been discontinued by the end of 1944. When the squadron became operational in September 1944, it had two Thunderbolt Mk.IIs and the following Mk.Is on strength: FL818, FL826, FL842, FL845, FL848, HB897, HB988, HB996, HB998, HD110, HD116, HD118, HD155 and HD161.

July following a fatal crash which occurred in another Thunderbolt unit. As a result, the Thunderbolts were grounded until the end of the month which nevertheless had seen the completion of over 370 hours of training on Thunderbolts.

Training resumed on the first day of August despite continuous problems with the supply of spares. The first bombing and strafing missions were carried out in the first week of the month. On 10 August 146 Squadron suffered its first death, when Sgt Geoffrey S. Cumberland crashed in HD111. Sgt Cumberland had taken off at 10.15, as No.2, for a practice formation flight. He made a steep turn to port, which brought him a little below and at an angle to his leader. He attempted to take up the correct position by carrying out a vertical climbing turn, but lost control. His aircraft crashed four miles SW of Yelahanka and caught fire. Cumberland had joined the squadron just a few days earlier, it being his first operational posting, and had flown only 12 hours on the type. Training was completed by the end of the month with around 800 hours flown and the squadron moved back to operate over Burma, carrying out *Rhubarbs* and armed reconnaissance missions. The first sorties were flown on 16th of the month when four Thunderbolts, led by the CO, took off for a strafing mission to Maylaik. However this mission became aborted because of heavy clouds over the targets which prevented any action. The next day the same operation was planned with eight aircraft but this was also aborted. The first real action occurred on the 25 August when three 'T-Bolts' led by F/L Raymond A.C Weir, the A Flight commander bombed and strafed the target (Maylaik) with efficiency. By the end of the month, about 60 sorties had been carried out. The squadron went to war mostly with Thunderbolt Mk.Is but also had four Thunderbolt Mk.IIs which exacerbated spare supply problems for the mechanics. After a couple of weeks, the squadron relinquished all its Mk.IIs for more MK.Is with the aim of simplifying maintenance.

In October, operational activity increased steadily with close to 200 sorties performed. However this was not achieved without loss, the squadron losing its first Thunderbolt in operations when F/Sgt Kenneth T. Orton flying HB996 was posted missing on 2 October. That day, at 12.15, four Thunderbolts led by F/O Benson (RCAF) took off to bomb and strafe Sanmyo. Heavy clouds were encountered at 16,000 feet, as well lightning storms north west of the target. The leader decided to abort the mission and the formation headed for base. At around 13.15 the aircraft entered thin cloud at 15,000 feet and, when they emerged, F/Sgt Orton was missing. It was his first operation and he had been with the squadron for less than two months. Three weeks later, the squadron lost its first Thunderbolt and pilot in combat – W/O 'Chuck' Verrier (RCAF) in FL842. Led by F/L Harold Benson (RCAF), eight Thunderbolts had taken off at 15.15 to attack Pantha village. The attack began at 16.10, all bombs falling in the village, which was also strafed, each Thunderbolt making four runs. However light flak located in the north east of the village was reported. During the raid, the aircraft flown by W/O Verrier was hit, while doing a strafing pass, Verrier having already dropped his bombs. The wreckage of his aircraft was observed the following day. Four aircraft had earlier that morning attempted to attack this target, but thick cloud between the Imphal Valley and Chindwin resulted in the pilots, including Verrier, returning to base early. By the end of the month, Raymond A.C. Weir took over the command of the squadron and led the unit in action during November. That month, the squadron continued its missions but lost only one Thunderbolt in action when, on the 11 November, ten Thunderbolts under the command of F/L Ray Walker, the new A Flight leader, an American serving in the RCAF, took off to attack Meitkila airfield and the target was duly attacked. On the return journey, W/O Edward R. Griffiths' Thunderbolt (FL845) experienced engine trouble, probably caused by small arms fire from the ground, and Griffiths called to advise his squadron mates that he would make an emergency landing. Later on, he was discovered to be a PoW being held at Rangoon. It was a bad period for the squadron which had also lost an aircraft on the ground the previous day, HB988, which had been destroyed by fire while the engine was run-up. Meitkila airfield caused the loss of another pilot in December – F/L 'Harb' Ivens (RCAF), the new B Flight commander, was leading nine aircraft when HD136 was hit by flak and crashed onto the target, but he was fortunate enough to survive, only to fall into Japanese hands. Becoming a PoW, he was freed in May 1945 with the liberation of Rangoon. No fewer than 315 sorties were performed in December, followed by a record of 430 sorties in January, this month being free from losses of any kind, as was February, despite over 300 sorties being carried out. In March, the squadron gave up its war-weary Thunderbolt Mk.Is for brand new Mk.IIs. The last patrols on Mk.Is were carried out on 13 March, marking an end to six months of operations on the Thunderbolt Mk.I which saw the completion of close to 1,700 sorties, a rather good record. One week later, 146 Squadron resumed operations with Mk.IIs.

Summary of the aircraft lost on Operations - 146 Squadron

Date	Pilot	S/N	Origin	Serial	Code	Fate
02.10.44	F/Sgt Kenneth T. **Orton**	RAF No. 1322067	RAF	**HB996**		†
24.10.44	W/O1 Charlie R. **Verrier**	Can./ R.101326	RCAF	**FL842**		†
11.11.44	W/O Edward R. **Griffiths**	RAF No. 1334202	RAF	**FL845**		PoW
11.12.44	F/L Herbert A. **Ivens**	Can./ J.10649	RCAF	**HD136**		PoW

Total: 4

After the loss of HD100, 'Terry' Marra chose HD118 as his personal mount. He was to carry out most of his ops flying this particular machine.

Summary of the aircraft lost by accident - 146 Squadron

Date	Pilot	S/N	Origin	Serial	Code	Fate
17.07.44	F/L Terence B. **Marra**	NZ403467	RNZAF	**HD101**		-
	F/O Livingstone A. W. **Kerr**	Can./ J.20379	RCAF	**FL744**		-
10.08.44	Sgt Geffrey S. **Cumberland**	RAF No. 1623541	RAF	**HD111**		†
10.11.44	-	-	-	**HB988**		-

Total: 4

No. 146 Squadron's Mk.Is lined up in October 1944 ready for an op with a full load of bombs under the wings. In the foreground is HD110/NA-L which was usually flown by Sydney A. Pickard. The Thunderbolts depicted wear an experimental identification scheme, partial white wing markings painted between the guns and the fuselage, while retaining full camouflage on the upper and lower surfaces.

No. 30 Squadron - code RS

Having started the war on Blenheims fitted with gun packs, 30 Squadron became a single-engined fighter unit in May 1941 flying Hurricanes. In June 1944, the squadron was still flying this type when it began its conversion to Thunderbolt Mk.Is at Yelahanka (India). The CO, who had recently been posted to the unit, was S/L Thomas A. Stevens who had served with 146 Squadron previously as a fight commander. The first 'T-bolts' arrived in the first week of July and the first flights took place on the 15th of the month, the CO making the first flight. By the end of the day, 26 pilots had completed their first solo on the Thunderbolt. On 28 July, all the P-47s were grounded following the crash of a 1670 CU Thunderbolt. By that time, around 275 hours had been logged on Thunderbolts. Flying practice resumed on 14 August, but this day was an unlucky one for the squadron, which lost two pilots and aeroplanes during training. The first of these was W/O Geoff Nowell who failed to return from a climb to height and who crashed five miles from Deyannalli. Later on, the Australian pilot W/O Keith J. Knodler was lost in similar circumstances. As a result, all height climbs were banned from the training program until further notice. The ban was lifted one week later on the 22nd. Despite these challenges, by the end of August most of the pilots had accumulated around 30 hours of flying time on the Thunderbolt. However, August ended with another loss – fortunately only a material one – when the aircraft flown by F/O Michael J. Kidd (RAAF), HD103, collided with the Thunderbolt flown by another Australian pilot, W/O Arnold Webster while landing after a squadron formation exercise. Webster's aircraft, FL813, was declared to be irreparable while HD103 was sent back to a MU for major work. Early in September, orders were received that the squadron, its conversion programme completed, was to move to Chittagong (India) after a three-week period at Arkonam where practice flying continued without incident. On 5 October, seventeen Thunderbolts flew to Chittagong. These were mainly Mk.I aircraft, though a handful of Mk.IIs were flown by the cadres, Flight leaders or the CO. The first operations were launched on 16 October, with four sorties carried out, two being on Mk.Is (HD156 - W/O Webster and HD177 - F/O William J.F. Dunlop, RCAF). By the end of the month 36 sorties were recorded, two-thirds of them with Mk.Is. The last week of October saw the arrival of further Mk.IIs, and 30 Squadron was able to replace the Mk.Is almost completely before the squadron moved to Cox's Bazar. Only two Mk.Is were retained for front line operations, HD114 and HD151, and these were only used for a couple of days on occasions when a Mk.II was not available for flying. The last Mk.I sortie was recorded on 19 November. In all, 30 Squadron completed 39 sorties on Thunderbolt Mk.Is, but was more active on Mk.IIs later on.

Summary of the aircraft lost by accident - 30 Squadron

Date	Pilot	S/N	Origin	Serial	Code	Fate
14.08.44	W/O Geoffrey G. **NEWELL**	RAF No. 1169512	RAF	**HB986**		†
	W/O Keith J. **KNOLDER**	Aus. 420211	RAAF	**HB995**		†
30.08.44	W/O Arnold C. **WEBSTER**	Aus. 408940	RAAF	**FL813**		-
	F/O Michael J. **KIDD**	Aus. 420345	RAAF	**HD103**		-

Total: 4

No. 30 Squadron made some use of the Thunderbolt Mk.I, but mainly for training. Here one, with squadron code letters 'RS' partially visible, undergoes an inspection. Mk.Is known to have served with the unit are FL813, FL834, HB986, HB995, HD103, HD108, HD114, HD115, HD126, HD134, HD151, HD156 and HD158.
(via J.F. Hamlin)

Flight mechanics prepare Thunderbolt Mk.Is of 30 Sqn for their next sortie from Cox's Bazar, India.

To describe the camouflage and markings of the Thunderbolt Mk.I in the Far East is not an easy task. Upon their arrival in India, they were sent to Maintenance Units where they were painted with Temperate Land Scheme colours: Dark Green/Dark Earth and Medium Sea Grey for the under surfaces. As most of the paint used by the RAF in the Far East was produced by local manufacturers, there was a variety in tone and quality and, therefore, no one standard existed. Further complicating matters is the fact that in many cases the under surfaces were left in American Light Grey to save time and money. Orange/Yellow strips were not painted on the leading edges. Only a handful of Thunderbolt Mk.Is received the large 32-inch SEAC roundels, most featured the 16-inch roundels. Dull Blue used for the centre of the roundel was often replaced by Sky, or a mix of colours close to it, as available photographs indicate. When a squadron took delivery of an aircraft its codes and individual aircraft letters were normally applied, although some units applied just the latter, but this practice was short-lived. It carried on within second-line units, however, right through until the end of the war. The position of these letters varied from squadron to squadron. The colour used was normally Sky, but sometimes this was seen as being too flashy alongside the Temperate Land Scheme colours and needed to be faded. Consequently, in many cases, letters were darkened with Dull Blue and White resulting in colours varying from Deep Sky to Light Grey-Blue, depending on the local mix. Thunderbolt Mk.I serials were generally painted in black, although some do appear in white (FL809). No. 135 Squadron is believed to have been the only squadron to use flight colours, a red propeller hub for A Flight and a blue one for B Flight, at least during the early months of its operations. Logically, though, the spinner of the aircraft flown by the CO (HB975) was left in NMF. Note also HB975's four mission markings, an irregular practice within squadrons as was individual noseart. Also unusual were the red and white chequers of 258 Sqn (HD133), but these were short-lived and totally disappeared when the identification bands were introduced in November 1944. Identification bands came about following concern over the ability to differentiate between radial engine Thunderbolts and Japanese opponents like the Ki-44 'Tojo'. A White cowl ring, wing and tail bands were then applied, identical to those painted on US Thunderbolts of the 80th FG operating in the CBI theatre. During a short period though, in October 1944, wing bands were painted in the region between the guns and the fuselage, and did not fully extend along the upper and under surfaces, and the tail band was very much thinner in width. Later on, the white paint on the rudder was removed from many aircraft for fear that it might disturb control balance, although some aircraft flew with the full band right up until the end of the war.

No. 34 Squadron - code EG

No.34 Squadron had been a bomber squadron since 1935 and served in the Far East since the beginning of the war. Since then, the only enemy it had faced had been the Japanese. In August 1943, the squadron became a fighter-bomber unit flying Hurricanes and participated in the heavy fighting in 1944. Even though operational activity decreased, it did not stop, and the squadron undertook its conversion onto the Thunderbolt at Wangjing under 910 Wing's authority, while continuing to carry out sorties. B Flight, with the CO, S/L John A. Busbridge who had led the unit since June 1944, were the first to convert. This took place from 9 March onwards, with ageing Mk.Is (FL832, FL846, HB968, HD105, HD110, HD118, HD128, HD151, HD165 being the aircraft most heavily used by 146 Squadron). This left A Flight to continue its support missions for the ground troops. On 17 March, F/L Noble took off with five other Thunderbolts to bomb and strafe Japanese positions north-east of Myindawgan, but W/O Whitling, flying HD165, had to return early due to engine trouble, leaving his squadron mates to continue the mission. The formation returned two hours later after the targets had been attacked, but no results were observed. A second bombing mission was carried out the next day with six Thunderbolts, led this time by P/O Hall, and was uneventful. During the last days of March, it was the turn of the pilots of A Flight to convert, and by the end of the month, with the progressive arrival of the Thunderbolt Mk.II which lasted into early April, the Mk.Is were sent to MUs. During that period, only one Thunderbolt was lost, FL835, during a training flight when F/Sgt John E.J. Auton struck a tree end of strip while taking off. The total number of sorties was 12.

Summary of the aircraft lost by accident - 34 Squadron

Date	Pilot	S/N	Origin	Serial	Code	Fate
25.03.45	F/Sgt John E.J. Auton	RAF No. 1508722	RAF	**FL835**		-

Total: 1

No. 79 Squadon - code NV

Under the leadership of S/L David O. Cunliffe, 79 Squadron arrived at Yelahanka on 26 May 1944 to convert to Thunderbolts. S/L Cunliffe had served for a long time in Far East and had been awarded the DFC while flying with 5 Squadron in 1943. The first aircraft arrived in mid-June but the first flight on Thunderbolts could not be carried out before mid-July, the intervening time having spent in lectures and cockpit drill, while flying training continued on the Hurricanes. The last Hurricanes eventually left on 6 July and one week later the first Thunderbolt solo was flown. Despite a shortage of spare parts and tools, flying hours could be accumulated almost at a normal rate. However because of an accident (not involving Thunderbolts of 79 Squadron), the Thunderbolts were grounded on 28th of the month, and training resumed on 14 August. At that time, S/L Cunliffe had been sent to the UK on a Fighter Leader Course, and command had been given temporary to F/L Kennetyh G. 'Gritty' Hemingway – Cunliffe never returned to the squadron and his post was taken by an Australian, S/L Roy D. May, in December. One week later, on 22 December, 79 Squadron first lost a pilot and aircraft (HD123) when F/O Francis N. O'Brien crashed from 30,000 feet, out of control, while on a height climb.

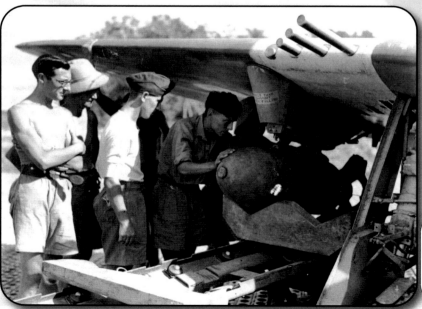

By mid-September, all the pilots except the new ones had completed their 30 hour course and the squadron moved on to Arkonam. Flying practice commencing from 20 September onwards. At the end of the month, the squadron had 29 pilots but only 13 Thunderbolts on hand. Another move took place on 19 October, to Manipur Road. A second accident occurred three days later, when the aircraft flown Lt 'Bill' Strike of the SAAF had a tyre burst on take-off for a long range tank test, necessitating a belly landing. The pilot escaped injuries, but HD157 was good only to be converted for spare parts.

The squadron was now ready for operations.

Armourers preparing to attach a 500-lb GP bomb to the wing pylon of a Thunderbolt in 1944. That was the classic load for the Thunderbolt in the Far East in the beginning of its operations as a fighter-bomber. Later on, napalm tanks would be used.

No.79 Squadron was not the only Thunderbolt unit to fly on both types, but it was the only one to have an equal proportion of Mk.I and Mk.II aircraft in its ranks. It was at that time part of 909 Wing. Operations began on the first day of November and, during that month, the squadron accomplished 157 sorties, around half by pilots flying Mk.Is. One Thunderbolt Mk.I was lost on 22 November when the Canadian Raymond E. Amey forgot to lower the landing gear and belly-landed during a transit flight from Imphal to the squadron's home base. In the next two months, the Mk.Is were progressively replaced by new Mk.II aircraft, and the number of sorties decreased slowly but surely – 75 of 272 in December, and 21 of 416 in January. The last two sorties were carried out on 15 January. In all, 79 Squadron performed 176 sorties on the Thunderbolt Mk.I, from over 2,600 sorties on Thunderbolts performed by the squadron overall. Known Thunderbolt Mk.Is used by the Squafron are: HB965, HB989, HB999, HD109, HD123, HD147, HD157, HD166, HD172, HD174.

Summary of the aircraft lost by accident - 79 Squadron

Date	Pilot	S/N	Origin	Serial	Code	Fate
22.08.44	F/O Francis N. **O'BRIEN**	RAF No. 146880	RAF	**HD123**		†
27.10.44	Lt William N. **STRIKE**	SAAF No. 329039V	SAAF	**HD157**		-
22.11.44	W/O Raymond E. **AMEY**	CAN./ R.134293	RCAF	**HB989**		-

Total: 3

No. 113 Squadron - code AD

This squadron begun the war as a bomber unit and fought in the Western Desert, Greece and Burma until 1943 when it was withdrawn to India to be converted to a fighter-bomber unit flying Hurricanes. It became operational on that type in October 1943 and was regularly used against the Japanese until April 1945 when it was converted to Thunderbolts. The last Hurricane sorties were completed on 5 April, and two days later the squadron, under the command of S/L Jack Rose, left Ondaw (Burma) where they were stationed. The unit flew to Wangjing (India) to take some old, not to say war-weary, Thunderbolt Mk.Is on charge. S/L Rose had been in charge of the squadron since the previous November and was a very experienced pilot, a veteran of the Battles of France and Britain (with Nos.3, 32 and 232 Sqns) who had been awarded the DFC. While a certain turnover of pilots was to be expected, half of the squadron pilot roster was changed that month making planning training difficult. Nevertheless, training commenced at once, though it started badly for the squadron. On the first training day, F/Sgt Robert Hunter crashed FL793 while performing a touch-and-go on his first solo on the type. There do not appear to have been any negative consequences for the pilot, but the

Thunderbolt was good only to be reduced to spare parts. Bad luck continued for 113 Squadron, which lost another aircraft and a pilot on the 15 April. Flight Sergeant David G. Dennett was posted missing during a training flight with HD148. A search was carried out and the wreckage quickly found with Dennett's body, and it was determined that he had been killed while attempting a force-landing after an engine failure. It must be said that serviceability of the aircraft remained poor during the month because of a lack of both spares and the correct tools to carry out maintenance, and also because of the age of the squadron's Thunderbolts. Nevertheless, the conversion was completed within two weeks, a short time when compared to other former Hurricane units, and by 20 April, the squadron moved back to Burma, to Kwentge. It was from here that the squadron took off for its first operational sorties on Thunderbolts four days later – one offensive reconnaissance made up of two aircraft, led by F/L Edward Slinger, early in the afternoon, followed by an offensive strike of six aircraft against Japanese positions, led P/O B.N. Read, in the middle of the afternoon. The next day, another uneventful strike was carried out. Until the end of the month, the squadron flew on average twice a day to contribute to the liberation of Rangoon, and in all 62 Thunderbolt sorties are recorded for April. These sometimes included the CO of 906 Wing, W/C R.N.H. Courtney, who had been the squadron's CO between January and September 1944. On the first day of May, a last offensive mission was performed by six aircraft with nothing to report. A couple of days later, two aircraft took off to deliver medical supplies putting an end to the first

Left, Jack Rose, who commanded 113 Sqn. He supervised the conversions of his pilots onto Thunderbolts, but, being at the end of his tour, did not fly them on operations himself. He had previously claimed three confirmed victories in France with 3 Sqn during May 1940.

Thunderbolt deployment for 113 Squadron, and a new CO, S/L Maurice Paddle, arrived at the squadron. With the new CO in place, the squadron was able to relinquish its old Mk.Is for new Mk.IIs early in June, and the pilots and mechanics had no regret in seeing the Mk.Is leaving for MUs.

Photos of 113 Sqn Thunderbolt Mk.Is are rare. The only known aircraft are FL793, FL843/Y, HD148 and HD173/N, but code letters A, C, D, E, H, K, L, N, R, S, T, X and ? (Question mark) were used by the squadron.

Summary of the aircraft lost by accident - 113 Squadron

Date	Pilot	S/N	Origin	Serial	Code	Fate
08.04.45	F/Sgt Robert **HUNTER**	RAF No. 573274	RAF	**FL793**		-
15.04.45	F/Sgt David G. **DENNETT**	RAF No. 1048316	RAF	**HD148**		†

Total: 2

123 Squadron - code XE

No.123 Squadron was reformed in May 1941 as a Spitfire unit in the UK, and served most of that year as a post-OTU unit until it was sent to the Middle East in April 1942. There, it served as a shadow unit for 80 Squadron and in October was sent to Iraq to protect the oilfields. Moving to the Western Egypt, the squadron began offensive missions in May 1943 but saw little action. It received new orders to move on again, this time to the Far East, in November 1943 under the command of S/L Alan J. McGregor, a former Battle of Britain veteran. The squadron began to be used regularly on operations in 1944, flying Hurricanes, mainly in the ground attack role, until May when the squadron stood down. For this reason it was naturally selected to convert to the

Thunderbolt. Conversion training began in mid-September and the squadron establishment was completed at the end of the month, the squadron being fully equipped with Thunderbolts Mk.Is. However the working-up period was lengthy and the squadron did not become operational until December 1944, by which time it was flying the more capable Thunderbolt Mk.II. Three Mk.Is, FL799 , HD106 and HD129, were kept as a back-up and hack for a part of January. In March the latter was sent to an MU, putting an end to the short and small-scale association between 123 Squadron and the Thunderbolt Mk.I. The training on Thunderbolt was conducted on the following known Mk.Is.: FL799, FL832, HD103, HD106.

No. 134 Squadron - code GQ

Under the command of S/L Donald K. McDonald, an Australian, 134 Sqn began its conversion to the Thunderbolt in July 1944. So far, it had been a Hurricane squadron which had served in UK, Russia and Middle East before moving to India at the end of 1943. McDonald was a very experienced pilot, recently awarded the DFC for his service with 261 Squadron, but he had flown with 130 Squadron in the UK, and then in Asia with 30, 135 and eventually 261 Squadrons. Early that month, a number of technician personnel were detached to 1670 CU in order to gain experience on Thunderbolts. On 23 August the first flights were recorded, the CO being the first to fly a Thunderbolt. More than 50 flights were carried out over the following days, but 134 Squadron lost its first Thunderbolt, HD100, when its pilot had to make a forced landing owing to an engine failure experienced during practice aerobatics. The pilot, Sgt David G. Wilde escaped major injuries. In one week, 134 Squadron flew close to 90 hours on Thunderbolts (some on Mk.IIs), but the main problem for the squadron was obtaining spare parts. Early in September, 134 Squadron continued its training with a few aircraft, none of them Mk.Is, these having been handed to 261 Squadron at the end of August. More aircraft were received during the month, with a few Mk.Is (known to include FL804/F, FL810/D, HB970, HB976, HB992/H, HD106, HD135/V, HD153/P and HD155). One of the latter group – HD106 – was damaged in a flying accident, though its pilot, the Australian Walter N. Godfrey escaped injury. The Thunderbolt was later repaired and served with 123 Squadron. However, 134 Squadron had to undertake its conversion course under the handicap of a lack of aircraft and spares, especially for the tyres, which proved to be fragile. This problem caused some minor accidents, but more importantly, led to the grounding of the aircraft involved for a while as there were no spares. Hence, the average of Thunderbolts available daily was no more than 12 throughout September. Because of these problems, the conversion course had to be shortened from 42 days to 36 as more squadrons were waiting for their own conversion. Despite this, over 750 hours were flown during the course which officially ended on 30 September.

On 6 October, 134 Squadron returned to Arkonam and continued to practice until the next move to Baigachi, in anticipation that the unit would go into action soon afterwards. However, the situation was less than satisfactory, with the squadron still flying a mixture of both Thunderbolt types. In fact, the squadron operated one flight which was mostly always equipped with the Mk.I, and the other flight equipped with the Mk.II. Consequently, when the squadron was put into action on 7 December, the Mk.Is were kept in reserve as far as possible, and only flew operations when a Mk.II was not available. However, two Mk.Is participated in the first mission carried out by 134 Squadron on Thunderbolts, a strafing mission to Mague airfield. Thunderbolts FL810, HB970, HB976 and HD135 were among the 12 aircraft which were despatched to strafe this airfield. During the month, the squadron carried out nearly 300 sorties without any major incidents, one third of sorties being flown by Mk.Is. However, maintenance on the two types was problematic due to the differences between each. This caused trouble and had an impact of the efficiency of the squadron. The situation was resolved in January as more Mk.II aircraft became available from MUs, and 134 Squadron was able to relinquish its Mk.Is for Mk.IIs, a last sortie being flown on 16 January. In all the squadron carried out 135 sorties on the Thunderbolt Mk.I.

Pilots of 134 Sqn watching squadron mates flying low over the airfield when the unit was still under training. Two mechanics can be seen servicing FL804/GQ-O which was later sent to the Middle East to serve with 73 OTU. It was one of the few Mk.Is sent there as a replacement aircraft in 1945.

Date	Pilot	S/N	Origin	Serial	Code	Fate
29.08.44	Sgt David G. **WILDE**	RAF No. 1622418	RAF	**HD100**		-
		Total: 1				

No. 258 Squadron - code ZT

No.258 Squadon had a chaotic existence before it began its conversion to the Thunderbolt at the end of summer 1944. The squadron was sent to Singapore with its Hurricanes in early 1942, and was involved in the disaster of the fall of Singapore. The squadron was re-formed in Ceylon soon afterwards and in 1943 was sent to India where the squadron fought as fighter-bomber unit. By summer 1944, it was ready to relinquish its ageing Hurricanes and was selected to fly Thunderbolts, the last flight on Hurricanes taking place on 5 August. By that time, 258 Squadron was led by S/L Neil Cameron and was based at Yelahanka. Neil Cameron was a veteran of the Battle of Britain and had fought in Russia in 1941 with 134 Squadron before fighting in the Middle East. Ground school on the Thunderbolt began in the next few days with 1670 CU aircraft and personnel. The first seven Thunderbolts Mk.Is arrived on 8 September, ferried by pilots of 134 Squadron, six more being delivered on the 10th of the month, and the last three (which were Mk.IIs) on 13 September. The training programme was accelerated and by the end of the month over 450 hours had been flown, though not without losses. During formation flying, Thunderbolts FL827, flown by W/O Ralph Vart, and HD141, flown by W/O Ralph V. Palesy (RAAF), collided in flight at 500 feet. Vart had tried to form up from below as briefed but had failed and when

A Thunderbolt Mk.I, FL792 of 258 Sqn, being serviced. In the early stages of the unit's Thunderbolt era, aircraft had red and white chequered cowlings, but these were soon abandoned.

he tried to join the formation from above, the accident occurred. Fortunately both pilots were able to bale out successfully though Palesy broke his leg, causing his repatriation to Australia. In October, 500 more hours were flown without incident to report regarding the Thunderbolt. On 2 November, the squadron lost two more Thunderbolts, both during a practice interception. The first (HD113), flown by F/O John Bellew, suffered an engine failure which obliged the pilot to make a forced landing, and 25 minutes later, it was the turn of P/O Robert D. King to face the same trouble with the same consequences. Both pilots escaped injuries. After investigation, it became clear that the two accidents had been caused by dirty fuel which had corroded the carburettor. These two Mk.Is were replaced by Mk.IIs, complicating the maintenance of the squadron's fleet, and now 258 Squadron had 11 Mk.Is and five Mk.IIs on its hands. However, the Mk.Is were the type which was used most during the month, completing 230 hours of the 310 hours flown in November.

Moving to Ratnap in Burma on 26 November, 258 Squadron began operations on 7 December. It had been decided to send 258 Squadron into combat with Mk.IIs only, but this could not be achieved because of lack of available aircraft, obliging the pilots to start operations on a mixture of both types. Indeed, things changed during December and while the squadron began operations with 13 Mk.Is, at the end of the month, this number had dropped to nine. Replacement aircraft continued to arrive in January and eventually the squadron was totally re-equipped with the Mk.II by the middle of the month. The last sorties on Mk.Is were recorded on 18 December. During two months of operations on Mk.Is, none were lost either in operations or in accidents in 217 sorties.

Summary of the aircraft lost by accident - 258 Squadron

Date	Pilot	S/N	Origin	Serial	Code	Fate
29.09.44	W/O Ralph **Vart**	RAF No. 1091379	RAF	**FL827**		-
	W/O Ralph V. **Palesy**	Aus. 413027	RAAF	**HD141**		-
02.11.44	F/O John **Bellew**	RAF No. 163030	RAF	**HD113**		-
	P/O Robert D. **King**	RAF No .184319	RAF	**HD179**		-

Total: 4

Above, seen here in Russia in 1941, Neil Cameron joined the RAF in May 1939. He served with Nos. 1 and 17 Sqns before being posted to 134 Sqn with which he fought in Russia. Later service was in the Middle East serving with Nos. 213 and 335 (Hellenic) Sqns. He was sent to India in October 1943 and was given command of 258 Sqn in February 1944.

Below, Russell K. Precians of New South Wales, Australia, had, like many of his fellow pilots, served for some time with 258 Sqn. Precians' tour started in October 1943, flying Hurricanes, and ended in August 1945 when he was repatriated. He completed 120 sorties, 70 of them on Thunderbolts.

These three photographs depict the series of changes that occurred to 258 Sqn's markings in the last weeks of 1944. At the top, the short-lived red/white cowlings. They were either deleted or not applied to new aircraft as seen on ZT-Z during October 1944. Thereafter, the introduction of white identification bands were applied to aircraft as seen on ZT-N (probably FL814). This photo also illustrates the harsh conditions pilots had to contend with in the Far East. No. 258 Squadron commenced operations with the following Thunderbolt Mk.Is: FL791, FL792/ZT-D, FL794, FL806/ZT-K, FL807, FL811/ZT-H, FL814/ZT-N, HB984/ZTS, HB991/ZT-X, HD129/ZT-B and HD133/ZT-Y. (*middle, via M. Schoeman*)

No. 261 Squadron - code FJ

No.261 Squadron was one of first two units to convert to the Thunderbolt. This Hurricane unit had been in the region since January 1943. In June 1944, 261 Squadron was led by S/L Richard E.A. Mason who had been in charge since May. The first flights took place on 24 June, and the squadron used the very first Thunderbolt Mk.Is with the Curtiss propeller, replaced by Thunderbolt D-22s by September. The training program started intensively and by the end of the month, 115 flights had been achieved. In July, training continued and a first Thunderbolt was lost when W/O Lawrence McGlinchey (RAAF) struck a tar barrel whilst taxying his aircraft, which was later declared damaged beyond economic repairs. Except for this accident, nothing noteworthy took place during the training phase and over 600 hours of training flight were carried out. In August, the pilots commenced the last part of their training (air-to-ground firing) and on the 15th of the month, 261 Squadron moved to Arkonam (India). Almost 400 hours were flown that month. By 2 September, the squadron was based at Kumbhirgram (India). It was there, just before becoming operational, that 261 Squadron experienced its second and last loss of a Mk.I, when returning from a sector recce on the 11 September, the Thunderbolt flown by F/Sgt Frederick W. Richard (HD178) was hit after landing by a Mk.II. Both were declared irreparable. Indeed, as for many others Thunderbolt units during the early stages of their service with the RAF, 261 Squadron had to fly a mixed fleet of Mk.Is and Mk.IIs, only half a dozen of the latter being actually on squadron charge.

On 16 September, the first mission on Thunderbolts was carried out, consisting of strafing and bombing a ground target, led by the CO. Of the three Thunderbolts which participated in this mission, only was a Mk I, HD117. By the end of September, over 100 sorties had been completed, half by Mk.Is, this proportion being reduced to one fifth the following month. The Mk.I was progressively replaced by new Mk.IIs. The last two Mk.I sorties were flown on 21 October and in all, 261 Squadron flew 77 sorties on Mk.Is. In October, the Mk.Is on charge were FL843/N, HB968/A, HB993, HD117/B, HD127, HD128, HD136, HD149 and HD165.

F/O Noel Faircloth, a New Zealander with the Thunderbolt Mk.I, FL742/FJ-B, he used to fly while serving with 261 Sqn. This squadron undertook training with the very first of the Mk.I models - the D-21. Some other D-21s used by the unit, up until they were replaced by D-22 models in September 1944, were: FL734/FJ-D, FL746/FJ-G, FL750, FL751/FJ-H, FL775/FJ-V, FL777/FJ-J and FL782/FJ-K. (*N. Faircloth via P. Sortehaug*)

Summary of the aircraft lost by accident - 261 Squadron

Date	Pilot	S/N	Origin	Serial	Code	Fate
10.07.44	W/O Lawrence **McGlinchey**	Aus. 420483	RAAF	**FL750**		-
11.09.44	F/Sgt Frederick W. **Rickard**	RAF No. 591517	RAF	**HD178**		-
		Total: 2				

WITH THE MISCELLANEOUS UNITS

Because of the lack of records, the movement cards having been destroyed at the end of the war, it is difficult to know with certainty with which units the Thunderbolt Mk.Is flew, except for the units already mentioned. What it is known is that the CCF (Check & Conversion Flight) at Mauripur used some Mk.Is between May and September 1944 when this unit was re-named 1331 CU (Conversion Unit) and re-located to Risalpur. The 1331 CU was formed at first to train crews for ferrying duties, hence the use of some Thunderbolts. FL731 and FL732, the first two Mk.Is, are known to have been part of the 1331 CU inventory, but also FL741. The later two were lost in a flying accident, without harm to the pilots. The Air Fighting Training Unit (AFTU) stationed at Armada Road used some Mk.Is as well. The AFTU was in charge of training Allied pilots in tactics practised by Japanese fighters and bombers in South East Asia and used a variety of aircraft types. Until it was disbanded in May 1945, the AFTU used at least FL732, FL749 and FL751, with FL749 being lost on 16 April 1945 during a training flight due to an engine failure in flight, obliging the pilot, Lt Rautenbach (SAAF) to make a forced landing. Otherwise, many Maintenance Units (MU), Repair & Salvage Units (RSU) or Ferry units (such as Ferry Control – FC, Staging Post – SP, Ferry Unit – FU) used a number a number of Mk.Is until the withdrawal of the type, some pilots being killed, such as the Canadian Francis Scandiffio (age 19 only) who was No.6 of a formation ferrying Thunderbolts to Yalahanka, a convoy led by a Beaufighter. The convoy entered cloud and when the aircraft emerged, Scandiffio was missing. All the other accidents involving a Mk.I were without major consequences for the pilots. Two more were lost while being serviced on the ground, like HD164, badly damaged by fire after the engine start and some flames shot out from turbo-superchager and extensively burned the fuselage. HD164 was later later converted to components.

Date	Pilot	S/N	Origin	Serial	Code	Unit	Fate
17.07.44	W/O Francis M. SCANDIFFIO	CAN./ R.93392	RCAF	HD163		21 FC	†
19.09.44	F/Sgt John K. VOWLES	RAF No. 1313955	RAF	FL732		1331 CU	-
15.11.44	*Caught fire starting up*	-	-	HD164		124 RSU	-
07.02.45	Lt Hugh LOCKHART-ROSS	SAAF No. 542438V	SAAF	FL797		10 FU	-
21.03.45	F/Sgt Arthur R. LEARY	RAF No. 1319910	RAF	FL741		1331 CU	-
16.04.45	Lt Johannes H. RAUTENBACH	SAAF No. 48116V	SAAF	FL749		AFTU	-
07.07.45	P/O William D. MCCORMICK	RAF No. 198170	RAF	FL740		135 RSU	-
06.10.45	W/O Charles W. PARCELL	RAF No. 1800766	RAF	HB998		36 SPFlt	-
02.12.45	F/O William D. SECKERSON	RAF No. 182111	RAF	HB993		2 SP	-

A mysterious photo of a Thunderbolt Mk.I. FL749/R has probably been incorrectly captioned as it is often referred to as a 5 Sqn aircraft at the end of 1944. At that time, though, all Thunderbolts were wearing white identification bands. However, from the various pilot's logbooks available, not just from 5 Sqn, and the ORBs, it can be determined that the D-21 models were generally used during the very first stages of the training process (June, July and August 1944), and so far no evidence can be found that they were used on combat operations. Another possibility, as indicated at the beginning of this study, is that 1670 CU was using, at the time, mostly D-21 Mk.Is with individual letters. FL749 could be one of them, or was maybe operated as an AFTU aircraft as these also carried single identifying letters.

†

IN MEMORIAM

Thunderbolt Mk.I

Name	Service No	Rank	Age	Origin	Date	Serial
Anson, Philip	RAF No. 1622305	F/Sgt	21	RAF	07.04.45	HD112
Carswell, John Jackson	RAF No. 1568844	Sgt	22	RAF	28.04.45	HD138
Cumberland, Geffrey Stephen	RAF No. 1623541	Sgt	21	RAF	10.08.44	HD111
Davies, Aubrey	RAF No. 1654041	Sgt	20	RAF	21.11.44	FL805
Dennett, David Greig	RAF No. 1048316	F/Sgt	22	RAF	15.04.45	HD148
Hart, Elton Budd	Can./ J.7903	F/L	22	RCAF	05.06.44	HB977
Knolder, Keith Jack	Aus. 420211	W/O	21	RAAF	14.08.44	HB995
Lapsley, Peter Rowland Challen	RAF No. 1474375	Sgt	20	RAF	27.07.44	FL767
Newell, Geoffrey George	RAF No. 185141	P/O	23	RAF	14.08.44	HB986
O'Brien, Francis Noel	RAF No. 146880	F/O	*n/k*	RAF	22.08.44	HD123
Orton, Kenneth Thomas	RAF No. 1322067	F/Sgt	*n/k*	RAF	02.10.44	HB996
Scandiffio, Francis Michael	Can./ J.88799	P/O	19	RCAF	17.07.44	HD163
Stevens, Paul Henry	RAF No. 1604434	F/Sgt	21	RAF	28.10.44	HB962
Tebby, Ronald John	RAF No. 1586928	F/Sgt	21	RAF	07.04.45	HB984
Verrier, Charlie Reginald	Can./ J.92099	P/O	23	RCAF	24.10.44	FL842
Wells, Richard Allen	RAF No. 772211	Sgt	22	RAF	30.01.45	FL802
Whiskin, Dennis Richard	RAF No. 1314711	W/O	22	RAF	28.03.45	HD158

Total: *17*

Australia: 1, Canada: 3, United Kingdom: 13

n/k: not known

Republic Thunderbolt Mk.I HD144
No. 73 Operational Training Unit (OTU)
Fayid (Egypt), autumn 1944

Republic Thunderbolt Mk. I FL809

No. 5 Squadron
Flight Sergeant John K. CROSS
Nazir (India), 1 April 1945

Republic Thunderbolt Mk. I HB975

No. 135 Squadron

Squadron Leader Leonard C.C. 'Lee' HAWKINS

Chittagong (India), autumn 1944

Republic Thunderbolt Mk.I FL848
No. 146 Squadron
Flying Officer Edgar N. WILSON (RNZAF)
Kumbhirgram (India), September 1944

Republic Thunderbolt Mk.I HD133
No. 258 Squadron
Pilot Officer Peter STEAD
Arkonam (India), autumn 1944

SQUADRONS! - The series

SQUADRONS!
No.3

The Supermarine
SPITFIRE Mk. V
in the Far East

USN AIRCRAFT
1922-1962

Vol.7:
Type Designation Letter
'F' (Pt-4)

Phil H. LISTEMANN

RAF, DOMINION & ALLIED SQUADRONS
AT WAR:
STUDY, HISTORY AND STATISTICS

No.137 Squadron
1941 - 1945

COMPILED BY
PHIL H. LISTEMANN
WITH
CHRIS THOMAS

Fighter Leaders
of the RAF, RAAF, RCAF, RNZAF & SAAF in WW2

Volume VII
IROG

Phil H. Listemann

SQUADRONS!
No.10

The North American
Mustang Mk. IV
in Western Europe

www.RAF-IN-COMBAT.com

- USN Aircraft 1922-1962 -
- Squadrons! -
- RAF, Dominion and Allied squadrons at War -
- Allied Wings -
- Famous squadrons of WW2 -
- Fighter Leaders -

RAF, DOMINION & ALLIED SQUADRON
AT WAR:
STUDY, HISTORY AND STATISTICS

No.151 (County of Kent) Squadron
1941 - 1945

ALLIED WINGS

SQUADRONS!
No.41

Famous Commonwealth Squadrons of WW2

No.453 (R.A.A.F) Squadron
1941-1945
Buffalo, Spitfire

The Bristol
Brigand

No.19

CANBERRA